Our Company

In 1928, at the age of twenty-two, Peter Beilenson began printing books on a small press in the basement of his parents' home in Larchmont, New York. Peter—and later, his wife, Edna—sought to create fine books that sold at "prices even a pauper could afford."

Today, still family owned and operated, Peter Pauper Press continues to honor our founders' legacy—and our customers' expectations—of beauty, quality, and value.

Designed by Tesslyn Pandarakalam

Illustrations copyright © Olivier Le Moal, used under license from Shutterstock.com.
Map © Cienpies Design, used under license from Shutterstock.com.

Copyright © 2016
Peter Pauper Press, Inc.
202 Mamaroneck Avenue
White Plains, NY 10601
All rights reserved
ISBN 978-1-4413-2049-0
Printed in China

Visit us at www.peterpauper.com

CONTENTS

Introduction 4
Tips to Start Your Search 5

Our Family Tree 6
Our Family 8
Our Marriage 12
Our Children 14
Our Grandchildren & Great Grandchildren 16
Parents (Her side) 20
Parents (His side) 22
Grandparents (Her side) 24
Grandparents (His side) 28

Our Ancestral Charts 32

Family Matters 41
Family Milestones: A Timeline 42
Our Family's World Today 44
Our Pets 46
Places Our Family Has Lived 48
Citizenship 52
Family World Map 56
Education 58
Occupations 60
Family Gatherings 62
Religious Milestones 64
What We Like 66
Events & Experiences That Have Brought Us Closer Together 70
What Makes Our Family Special 72
Family Health 74
Family Treasures 76
Military Service 78
Family We Miss 80

Family Photographs, Mementos, & Additional Notes 82
Sources of Information 100

Introduction

Family matters. Climb into your family tree and start exploring its limbs and branches! Genealogy may seem daunting, but this friendly organizer will enable you to begin recording the story of your family right away, starting with basic information on your immediate family, close family members, and your forebears. You'll also find places to record citizenship information, education, professions, family traits, family favorites, and more. Pages in the back allow you to add more notes, or paste in documents, mementos, and photographs. Leaf through this book, select a section, and begin! In the end you'll have a keepsake to preserve for your family now and for generations to come.

Tips to Start Your Search

- Fill in information with a pencil first.

- Write each person's full name in the normal order, and include maiden or former names. Capitalize surnames (last names or family names).

- Common abbreviations you may wish to use in the "Notes" sections: b. = birth; m. = marriage (If someone is married more than once, use m1, and m2.); d. = death; bp. = birthplace; mp. = marriage place; dp. = death place.

- Record addresses & address abbreviations as clearly & accurately as possible.

- Write out dates like so: date, month (use three letters only except for June), year: 7 Nov 1856, 23 Jan 1947, 1 June 2015 (spell out June so it is not confused with Jan), 4 Jul 1776.

- Look for information among family records and documents, deeds, military records, newspaper accounts and notices, school records, family Bibles, photographs (check for dates on front and back), scrapbooks, etc.

- Document your sources of information in the back of this book, in case others wish to consult your sources, or if you wish to return to your findings.

OUR FAMILY TREE

OUR FAMILY

Full name ....
Date & place of birth ....
Notes ....
....
....
....
....
....

Full name ....
Date & place of birth ....
Notes ....
....
....
....
....
....

Full name ....
Date & place of birth ....
Notes ....
....
....
....
....
....

Full name ....
Date & place of birth ....
Notes ....
....
....
....
....
....

Full name ....

Date & place of birth ....

Notes ....

....

....

....

....

....

Full name ....

Date & place of birth ....

Notes ....

....

....

....

....

....

Full name ....

Date & place of birth ....

Notes ....

....

....

....

....

....

Full name ....

Date & place of birth ....

Notes ....

....

....

....

....

....

Our Family

Full name ....
Date & place of birth ....
Notes ....
....
....
....
....
....

Full name ....
Date & place of birth ....
Notes ....
....
....
....
....
....

Full name ....
Date & place of birth ....
Notes ....
....
....
....
....
....

Full name ....
Date & place of birth ....
Notes ....
....
....
....
....
....

Full name ....

Date & place of birth ....

Notes ....

....

....

....

....

Full name ....

Date & place of birth ....

Notes ....

....

....

....

....

Full name ....

Date & place of birth ....

Notes ....

....

....

....

....

Full name ....

Date & place of birth ....

Notes ....

....

....

....

....

Our Marriage

Full name ....

Date & place of birth ....

Notes ....

....

....

Full name ....

Date & place of birth ....

Notes ....

....

....

Date of wedding ....

Place ....

Married by ....

Marriage certificate number ....

Notes ....

Photographs & mementos

Our Children

Full name ....
Date & place of birth ....
Notes ....
....
....
....
....
....
....
....
....

Full name ....
Date & place of birth ....
Notes ....
....
....
....
....
....
....
....
....

Full name ....
Date & place of birth ....
Notes ....
....
....
....
....
....
....
....
....

Full name ....
Date & place of birth ....
Notes ....
....
....
....
....
....
....
....
....

Full name ....
Date & place of birth ....
Notes ....
....
....
....
....
....
....
....
....

Full name ....
Date & place of birth ....
Notes ....
....
....
....
....
....
....
....
....

OUR GRANDCHILDREN & GREAT GRANDCHILDREN

Full name ....
Date & place of birth ....
Parents' names ....
Notes ....
....
....

Full name ....
Date & place of birth ....
Parents' names ....
Notes ....
....
....

Full name ....
Date & place of birth ....
Parents' names ....
Notes ....
....
....

Full name ....
Date & place of birth ....
Parents' names ....
Notes ....
....
....

Full name ....
Date & place of birth ....
Parents' names ....
Notes ....
....
....

Full name ....
Date & place of birth ....
Parents' names ....
Notes ....
....
....

Full name ....
Date & place of birth ....
Parents' names ....
Notes ....
....
....

Full name ....
Date & place of birth ....
Parents' names ....
Notes ....
....
....

Full name ....
Date & place of birth ....
Parent's names ....
Notes ....
....
....

Full name ....
Date & place of birth ....
Parents' names ....
Notes ....
....
....

Our Grandchildren & Great Grandchildren

Full name ....
Date & place of birth ....
Parents' names ....
Notes ....
....
....

Full name ....
Date & place of birth ....
Parents' names ....
Notes ....
....
....

Full name ....
Date & place of birth ....
Parents' names ....
Notes ....
....
....

Full name ....
Date & place of birth ....
Parents' names ....
Notes ....
....
....

Full name ....
Date & place of birth ....
Parents' names ....
Notes ....
....
....

Full name ....
Date & place of birth ....
Parents' names ....
Notes ....
....
....

Full name ....
Date & place of birth ....
Parents' names ....
Notes ....
....
....

Full name ....
Date & place of birth ....
Parents' names ....
Notes ....
....
....

Full name ....
Date & place of birth ....
Parents' names ....
Notes ....
....
....

Full name ....
Date & place of birth ....
Parents' names ....
Notes ....
....
....

Parents (Her Side)

Father's full name ....
Date & place of birth ....
Notes about father's family ....

Mother's full name ....
Date & place of birth ....
Notes about mother's family ....

Parents (His Side)

Father's full name ....

Date & place of birth ....

Notes about father's family ....

Mother's full name ....
Date & place of birth ....
Notes about mother's family ....

Grandparents (Her Side)

Grandfather's full name ....

Date & place of birth ....

Notes about grandfather's family ....

....
....
....
....
....
....
....
....
....
....
....
....
....
....
....
....
....
....
....
....
....
....
....
....
....
....
....

Grandmother's full name ....
Date & place of birth ....
Notes about grandmother's family ....

Grandparents (Her Side)

Grandfather's full name ....
Date & place of birth ....
Notes about grandfather's family ....

Grandmother's full name ....

Date & place of birth ....

Notes about grandmother's family ....

....
....
....
....
....
....
....
....
....
....
....
....
....
....
....
....
....
....
....
....
....
....
....
....
....
....
....
....
....
....

GRANDPARENTS (HIS SIDE)

Grandfather's full name ....

Date & place of birth ....

Notes about grandfather's family ....

Grandmother's full name ....

Date & place of birth ....

Notes about grandmother's family ....

Grandparents (His Side)

Grandfather's full name..

Date & place of birth ....

Notes about grandfather's family ....

Grandmother's full name ....

Date & place of birth ....

Notes about grandmother's family ....

Ancestral Chart (Hers)

1. **Full name** ....
Date & place of birth ....
Notes ....
....
....
....

4. Grandfather's full name

Date & place of birth

Notes ....
....
....
....

2. Father's full name

Date & place of birth

Notes ....
....
....
....

5. Grandmother's full name

Date & place of birth

Notes ....
....
....
....

6. Grandfather's full name

Date & place of birth

Notes ....
....
....
....

3. Mother's full name

Date & place of birth

Notes ....
....
....
....

7. Grandmother's full name

Date & place of birth

Notes ....
....
....
....

Ancestral Chart (Hers)

8. Great Grandfather's full name

Date & place of birth

Notes

9. Great Grandmother's full name

Date & place of birth

Notes

10. Great Grandfather's full name

Date & place of birth

Notes

11. Great Grandmother's full name

Date & place of birth

Notes

12. Great Grandfather's full name

Date & place of birth

Notes

13. Great Grandmother's full name

Date & place of birth

Notes

14. Great Grandfather's full name

Date & place of birth

Notes

15. Great Grandmother's full name

Date & place of birth

Notes

16. Great, Great Grandfather's full name

17. Great, Great Grandmother's full name

18. Great, Great Grandfather's full name

19. Great, Great Grandmother's full name

20. Great, Great Grandfather's full name

21. Great, Great Grandmother's full name

22. Great, Great Grandfather's full name

23. Great, Great Grandmother's full name

24. Great, Great Grandfather's full name

25. Great, Great Grandmother's full name

26. Great, Great Grandfather's full name

27. Great, Great Grandmother's full name

28. Great, Great Grandfather's full name

29. Great, Great Grandmother's full name

30. Great, Great Grandfather's full name

31. Great, Great Grandmother's full name

32. Great, Great, Great Grandfather ....
33. Great, Great, Great Grandmother ....

34. Great, Great, Great Grandfather ....
35. Great, Great, Great Grandmother ....

36. Great, Great, Great Grandfather ....
37. Great, Great, Great Grandmother ....

38. Great, Great, Great Grandfather ....
39. Great, Great, Great Grandmother ....

40. Great, Great, Great Grandfather ....
41. Great, Great, Great Grandmother ....

42. Great, Great, Great Grandfather ....
43. Great, Great, Great Grandmother ....

44. Great, Great, Great Grandfather ....
45. Great, Great, Great Grandmother ....

46. Great, Great, Great Grandfather ....
47. Great, Great, Great Grandmother ....

48. Great, Great, Great Grandfather ....
49. Great, Great, Great Grandmother ....

50. Great, Great, Great Grandfather ....
51. Great, Great, Great Grandmother ....

52. Great, Great, Great Grandfather ....
53. Great, Great, Great Grandmother ....

54. Great, Great, Great Grandfather ....
55. Great, Great, Great Grandmother ....

56. Great, Great, Great Grandfather ....
57. Great, Great, Great Grandmother ....

58. Great, Great, Great Grandfather ....
59. Great, Great, Great Grandmother ....

60. Great, Great, Great Grandfather ....
61. Great, Great, Great Grandmother ....

62. Great, Great, Great Grandfather ....
63. Great, Great, Great Grandmother ....

Ancestral Chart (His)

1. **Full name** ....
Date & place of birth ....
Notes ....
....
....
....

2. Father's full name

Date & place of birth

Notes ....
....
....
....

3. Mother's full name

Date & place of birth

Notes ....
....
....
....

4. Grandfather's full name

Date & place of birth

Notes ....
....
....
....

5. Grandmother's full name

Date & place of birth

Notes ....
....
....
....

6. Grandfather's full name

Date & place of birth

Notes ....
....
....
....

7. Grandmother's full name

Date & place of birth

Notes ....
....
....
....

Ancestral Chart (His)

8. Great Grandfather's full name

Date & place of birth

Notes

9. Great Grandmother's full name

Date & place of birth

Notes

16. Great, Great Grandfather's full name

17. Great, Great Grandmother's full name

18. Great, Great Grandfather's full name

19. Great, Great Grandmother's full name

10. Great Grandfather's full name

Date & place of birth

Notes

11. Great Grandmother's full name

Date & place of birth

Notes

20. Great, Great Grandfather's full name

21. Great, Great Grandmother's full name

22. Great, Great Grandfather's full name

23. Great, Great Grandmother's full name

12. Great Grandfather's full name

Date & place of birth

Notes

13. Great Grandmother's full name

Date & place of birth

Notes

24. Great, Great Grandfather's full name

25. Great, Great Grandmother's full name

26. Great, Great Grandfather's full name

27. Great, Great Grandmother's full name

14. Great Grandfather's full name

Date & place of birth

Notes

15. Great Grandmother's full name

Date & place of birth

Notes

28. Great, Great Grandfather's full name

29. Great, Great Grandmother's full name

30. Great, Great Grandfather's full name

31. Great, Great Grandmother's full name

32. Great, Great, Great Grandfather ....
33. Great, Great, Great Grandmother ....

34. Great, Great, Great Grandfather ....
35. Great, Great, Great Grandmother ....

36. Great, Great, Great Grandfather ....
37. Great, Great, Great Grandmother ....

38. Great, Great, Great Grandfather ....
39. Great, Great, Great Grandmother ....

40. Great, Great, Great Grandfather ....
41. Great, Great, Great Grandmother ....

42. Great, Great, Great Grandfather ....
43. Great, Great, Great Grandmother ....

44. Great, Great, Great Grandfather ....
45. Great, Great, Great Grandmother ....

46. Great, Great, Great Grandfather ....
47. Great, Great, Great Grandmother ....

48. Great, Great, Great Grandfather ....
49. Great, Great, Great Grandmother ....

50. Great, Great, Great Grandfather ....
51. Great, Great, Great Grandmother ....

52. Great, Great, Great Grandfather ....
53. Great, Great, Great Grandmother ....

54. Great, Great, Great Grandfather ....
55. Great, Great, Great Grandmother ....

56. Great, Great, Great Grandfather ....
57. Great, Great, Great Grandmother ....

58. Great, Great, Great Grandfather ....
59. Great, Great, Great Grandmother ....

60. Great, Great, Great Grandfather ....
61. Great, Great, Great Grandmother ....

62. Great, Great, Great Grandfather ....
63. Great, Great, Great Grandmother ....

Additional Ancestry Notes

FAMILY MILESTONES: A TIMELINE

You may use this timeline as an extra way to record events that are part of your family history, such as when you and your spouse met, when children were born or started school, when you acquired your first home, car, or pet, etc.

Date... Date...
Event .... **Event** ....

Date... Date...
Event .... **Event** ....

Date... Date...
Event .... **Event** ....

Date... Date...
Event .... **Event** ....

Date... Date...
Event .... **Event** ....

Date ....
Event ....

Date ....
Event ....

Date ....
Event ....

Date ....
Event ....

Date ....
Event ....

Date ....
Event ....

Date ....
Event ....

Date ....
Event ....

Date ....
Event ....

Date ....
Event ....

Our Family's World Today

Use this space to record details of daily life for posterity, such as the prices of grocery items or fuel, television shows you watch (& maybe how you're watching them), music you enjoy, etc.

OUR PETS

Pet name ....
Type of pet ....
When it joined the family ....
Notes ....
....
....
....

Pet name ....
Type of pet ....
When it joined the family ....
Notes ....
....
....
....

Pet name ....
Type of pet ....
When it joined the family ....
Notes ....
....
....
....

Pet name ....
Type of pet ....
When it joined the family ....
Notes ....
....
....
....

Pet name ....
Type of pet ....
When it joined the family ....
Notes ....
....
....
....

Pet name ....
Type of pet ....
When it joined the family ....
Notes ....
....
....
....

Pet name ....
Type of pet ....
When it joined the family ....
Notes ....
....
....
....

Pet name ....
Type of pet ....
When it joined the family ....
Notes ....
....
....
....

Places Our Family Has Lived

If you've moved, you may wish to keep a record of former addresses & notes about each home.

Address ....

Owned/rented ....

When we lived there ....

Notes ....

....

....

....

....

....

....

....

....

....

....

....

....

....

....

....

Photographs

Address
Owned/rented
When we lived there
Notes

Photographs

Places Our Family Has Lived

Address ....

Owned/rented ....

When we lived there ....

Notes ....

....

....

....

....

....

....

....

....

....

....

....

....

....

....

....

....

....

Photographs

Address ....
Owned/rented ....
When we lived there ....
Notes ....
....
....
....
....
....
....
....
....
....
....
....
....
....
....
....

Photographs

CITIZENSHIP (HER SIDE)

List any countries from which your family originated. You might also note where they came to reside or are now residing.

Name ....
Original country ....
Emigration date ....
Where they came to live ....
Notes ....
....
....
....
....

Name ....
Original country ....
Emigration date ....
Where they came to live ....
Notes ....
....
....
....
....

Name ....
Original country ....
Emigration date ....
Where they came to live ....
Notes ....
....
....
....
....

Name ....
Original country ....
Emigration date ....
Where they came to live ....
Notes ....
....
....
....
....

Name ....
Original country ....
Emigration date ....
Where they came to live ....
Notes ....
....
....
....
....

Name ....
Original country ....
Emigration date ....
Where they came to live ....
Notes ....
....
....
....
....

CITIZENSHIP (HIS SIDE)

List any countries from which your family originated. You might also note where they came to reside or are now residing.

Name ....
Original country ....
Emigration date ....
Where they came to live ....
Notes ....
....
....
....
....

Name ....
Original country ....
Emigration date ....
Where they came to live ....
Notes ....
....
....
....
....

Name ....
Original country ....
Emigration date ....
Where they came to live ....
Notes ....
....
....
....
....

Name ....
Original country ....
Emigration date ....
Where they came to live ....
Notes ....
....
....
....
....

Name ....
Original country ....
Emigration date ....
Where they came to live ....
Notes ....
....
....
....
....

Name ....
Original country ....
Emigration date ....
Where they came to live ....
Notes ....
....
....
....
....

Family World Map

Where in the world has your family been? You can use this map to note where family has lived in the past or where you live now. Tip: Use different colored pencils for each purpose.

....
....
....
....
....

....
....
....
....
....
....
....

....
....
....
....
....
....
....
....
....
....
....

....
....
....
....
....

Education

Make notes about family members' education here.

Name ....
Institution ....
Dates of attendance ....
Degree, certification, etc. ....
Notes ....
....
....
....

Name ....
Institution ....
Dates of attendance ....
Degree, certification, etc. ....
Notes ....
....
....
....

Name ....
Institution ....
Dates of attendance ....
Degree, certification, etc. ....
Notes ....
....
....
....

Name ....
Institution ....
Dates of attendance ....
Degree, certification, etc. ....
Notes ....
....
....
....

Name ....
Institution ....
Dates of attendance ....
Degree, certification, etc. ....
Notes ....
....
....
....

Name ....
Institution ....
Dates of attendance ....
Degree, certification, etc. ....
Notes ....
....
....
....

Name ....
Institution ....
Dates of attendance ....
Degree, certification, etc. ....
Notes ....
....
....
....

Name ....
Institution ....
Dates of attendance ....
Degree, certification, etc. ....
Notes ....
....
....
....

Occupations

What kinds of employment have family members been engaged in? Have any had their own businesses? Make note of them here.

Name ....

Occupation ....

Dates ....

Notes ....

....

....

....

....

Name ....

Occupation ....

Dates ....

Notes ....

....

....

....

....

Name ....

Occupation ....

Dates ....

Notes ....

....

....

....

....

Name ....

Occupation ....

Dates ....

Notes ....

....

....

....

....

Name ....
Occupation ....
Dates ....
Notes ....

....

....

....

....

Name ....
Occupation ....
Dates ....
Notes ....

....

....

....

....

Name ....
Occupation ....
Dates ....
Notes ....

....

....

....

....

Name ....
Occupation ....
Dates ....
Notes ....

....

....

....

....

Family Gatherings

Does your family have an annual reunion? Are there other special gatherings or vacations you'd like to remember? Record them here.

Occasion ....

Date ....

Place ....

Notes ....

....

....

....

....

Occasion ....

Date ....

Place ....

Notes ....

....

....

....

....

Occasion ....

Date ....

Place ....

Notes ....

....

....

....

....

Occasion ....

Date ....

Place ....

Notes ....

....

....

....

....

Occasion ....
Date ....
Place ....
Notes ....
....
....
....
....

Occasion ....
Date ....
Place ....
Notes ....
....
....
....
....

Occasion ....
Date ....
Place ....
Notes ....
....
....
....
....

Occasion ....
Date ....
Place ....
Notes ....
....
....
....
....

Religious Milestones

Record details about religious occasions and celebrations here.

Name ....
Occasion ....
Date ....
Place ....
Notes ....
....
....
....

Name ....
Occasion ....
Date ....
Place ....
Notes ....
....
....
....

Name ....
Occasion ....
Date ....
Place ....
Notes ....
....
....
....

Name ....
Occasion ....
Date ....
Place ....
Notes ....
....
....
....

Name ....
Occasion ....
Date ....
Place ....
Notes ....
....
....
....

Name ....
Occasion ....
Date ....
Place ....
Notes ....
....
....
....

Name ....
Occasion ....
Date ....
Place ....
Notes ....
....
....
....

Name ....
Occasion ....
Date ....
Place ....
Notes ....
....
....
....

What We Like

Here is where you can record family pastimes, favorite stories and anecdotes, recipes, and more.

What We Like

Events & Experiences

Describe events that have happened in your world, and how they've affected your family.

Event ....
Date ....
Notes ....
....
....
....

Event ....
Date ....
Notes ....
....
....
....

Event ....
Date ....
Notes ....
....
....
....

Event ....
Date ....
Notes ....
....
....
....

Event ....
Date ....
Notes ....
....
....
....

That Have Brought Us Closer Together

Event ....
Date ....
Notes ....
....
....
....

Event ....
Date ....
Notes ....
....
....
....

Event ....
Date ....
Notes ....
....
....
....

Event ....
Date ....
Notes ....
....
....
....

Event ....
Date ....
Notes ....
....
....
....

WHAT MAKES OUR FAMILY SPECIAL

Is anyone left-handed? Does anyone have red hair? How about eye color? Dimples? Write down those traits here.

Name ....
Notes ....
....
....
....
....

Name ....
Notes ....
....
....
....
....

Name ....
Notes ....
....
....
....
....

Name ....
Notes ....
....
....
....
....

Name ....
Notes ....
....
....
....
....

Name ....
Notes ....
....
....
....
....

Name ....
Notes ....
....
....
....
....

Name ....
Notes ....
....
....
....
....

Name ....
Notes ....
....
....
....
....

Name ....
Notes ....
....
....
....
....

Family Health

Make note of family health information, blood types, conditions, and so forth that might be useful for future family members to know.

Name ....

Notes ....

....

....

....

....

Name ....

Notes ....

....

....

....

....

Name ....

Notes ....

....

....

....

....

Name ....

Notes ....

....

....

....

....

Name ....

Notes ....

....

....

....

....

Name ....
Notes ....
....
....
....
....

Name ....
Notes ....
....
....
....
....

Name ....
Notes ....
....
....
....
....

Name ....
Notes ....
....
....
....
....

Name ....
Notes ....
....
....
....
....

Family Treasures

List any family heirlooms and antiques that may have been passed down, as well as any other collectibles or treasured items.

Item ....
Location ....
Notes ....
....
....
....

Item ....
Location ....
Notes ....
....
....
....

Item ....
Location ....
Notes ....
....
....
....

Item ....
Location ....
Notes ....
....
....
....

Item ....
Location ....
Notes ....
....
....
....

Item
Location
Notes

Item
Location
Notes

Item
Location
Notes

Item
Location
Notes

Item
Location
Notes

MILITARY SERVICE

Here is a place in which you can record information about family members who have served their country.

Name ....
Service ....
Unit/Regiment ....
Rank/Grade ....
Dates ....
Notes ....
....
....
....
....
....

Name ....
Service ....
Unit/Regiment ....
Rank/Grade ....
Dates ....
Notes ....
....
....
....
....
....

Name ....
Service ....
Unit/Regiment ....
Rank/Grade ....
Dates ....
Notes ....
....
....
....
....
....

Name ....
Service ....
Unit/Regiment ....
Rank/Grade ....
Dates ....
Notes ....
....
....
....
....
....

Name ....
Service ....
Unit/Regiment ....
Rank/Grade ....
Dates ....
Notes ....
....
....
....
....
....

Name ....
Service ....
Unit/Regiment ....
Rank/Grade ....
Dates ....
Notes ....
....
....
....
....
....

FAMILY WE MISS

This is a place for remembrances of relatives past. Record those special memories here.

Name ....
Date of birth .... Date of death ....
Notes ....
....
....
....

Name ....
Date of birth .... Date of death ....
Notes ....
....
....
....

Name ....
Date of birth .... Date of death ....
Notes ....
....
....
....

Name ....
Date of birth .... Date of death ....
Notes ....
....
....
....

Name ....
Date of birth .... Date of death ....
Notes ....
....
....
....

Name ....
Date of birth ....Date of death ....
Notes ....
....
....
....

Name ....
Date of birth ....Date of death ....
Notes ....
....
....
....

Name ....
Date of birth ....Date of death ....
Notes ....
....
....
....

Name ....
Date of birth ....Date of death ....
Notes ....
....
....
....

Name ....
Date of birth ....Date of death ....
Notes ....
....
....
....

Family Photographs, Mementos,

Paste keepsake documents, photos, and other memorabilia in this section. Write in your own captions, or use the lined space to record more information about your family.

& Additional Notes

Family Photographs, Mementos,

& Additional Notes

Family Photographs, Mementos,

& Additional Notes

Family Photographs, Mementos,

& Additional Notes

Family Photographs, Mementos,

& Additional Notes

Family Photographs, Mementos,

& Additional Notes

Family Photographs, Mementos,

& Additional Notes

Family Photographs, Mementos,

& Additional Notes

Family Photographs, Mementos,

& Additional Notes

Sources of Information

Record the sources through which you located information about your family history for future reference.

Date	Description of Source	Location of Source	Notes

Date	Description of Source	Location of Source	Notes

Sources of Information

Record the sources through which you located information about your family history for future reference.

Date	Description of Source	Location of Source	Notes

Date	Description of Source	Location of Source	Notes

Sources of Information

Record the sources through which you located information about your family history for future reference.

Date	Description of Source	Location of Source	Notes